I never knew how to put my feelings into words, at least words that made sense when speaking. I always thought I was burdening people with my words so I never spoke them, not to anyone I could scare away at least. I spoke to my stuffed animals and my dog, but apart from them I refused to have any emotional human interactions. Sure I would cry and I knew why, but I never had the words to explain why.

The words my friends used to describe not getting a dog or the new Barbie never really felt right to describe the way non-consensual hands traced my body. There had to be other words, ones just for me, ones to label the things I felt so I could finally store them away. But no dictionary ever gave me the words I needed. No book gave me the sentences and no one experience could be described by the formal english dialect.

So I took to poetry, to truly explain the things I felt, and to be honest with you there are still images trapped in my mind which no level of metaphors or personification could describe, but for the things poetry has cured I am forever grateful.

So this book is for the girls who are expected to know how they feel but never can find the right label... you're not alone and I love you. So I ask you to come with me and step into a world where words dance on the edge of emotions, where every stanza is a brushstroke painting vivid scenes of love, loss, and the kaleidoscope of human experience. In this enchanting collection of poetry, each verse whispers secrets of the heart, exploring the depths of longing and the heights of joy. Through lyrical expressions and evocative imagery, I invite you to wander through landscapes of nostalgia and dreams, where every poem is a journey into the intricacies of the soul.

From tender reflections on nature's beauty to raw, unfiltered confessions of pain, these poems traverse the spectrum of human feelings with grace and honesty. They capture fleeting moments of serenity and turmoil, weaving a tapestry of emotions that I hope will resonate with you on a profound level. Whether pondering the mysteries of existence or celebrating the resilience of the human spirit, each of my poems offers a glimpse into my own heart, and I invite you, dear reader, to contemplate your own experiences and find solace in shared humanity.

This collection is a testament to the power of the language that heals, uplifts, and connects. I invite you to pause, to linger, and to savour the richness of language that speaks directly to the soul. As you turn the pages, you will discover a treasure trove of poetic gems that illuminate the beauty of life's fleeting moments and the

enduring power of the written word. Embrace the journey through this tapestry of emotions and let each poem resonate with your own personal narrative, for in these verses lies the magic of poetry—timeless, evocative, and deeply moving.

Chapters

The lady in me……….
The little girl in me……..
A part of me…….
The desire in me…….
The curiosity in me…….
The powerful part of me…..

The Lady In Me

Some of us think that holding on makes us strong; but
sometimes it is letting go
~ Hermann Hesse

The lady in me stands tall and bold,
A fortress of strength, resilient and true.
She walks with purpose, confident and controlled,
In a world that often underestimates what she can do.

Her voice, a beacon of wisdom and grace,
Echoes with tales of battles fought and won.
Yet in the depths of her heart's secret place,
Lies a longing for the innocence undone.

She wears her dignity like armour,
Refusing to yield to the tides of dismay.
But behind her composed demeanour,
Lies the echo of childhood's playful display.

In her eyes, a flicker of wistful yearning,
For moments of whimsy and pure delight.
To run barefoot through fields, carefree and unerring,
To reclaim the innocence lost in life's relentless flight.

The lady in me, strong yet tender,
Carries the weight of her dreams untold.
In her soul, the essence of a girl's surrender,
Yearning for a time when being herself was gold.

I was an ocean full of beauty and love,
But you were afraid of the sharks

Would you hold my hand
Even if it's sweaty?
Would you give me your sweater
Even if it means you'll be cold?
Would you hold me tight
While I'm breaking down?
Will you kiss me
Before going to sleep?
Will you remind me
Of how much you love me?
Are you willing to wipe my tears
And let me know everything is going to be okay?
Are you willing to drive hours
Just to get away from reality?
Are you willing to love me
Even at my worst ?

I wonder what's keeping me from speaking
Is it the tears coming from my eyes
Or is it the anxiety that makes it hard to breathe
Is it the fact i keep saying "i'm fine"
Or maybe it's the overwhelming fear they'll find out i'm
not
I tell them don't worry because i'm not their problem
But i am THE problem
Just not the kind they should worry about
I wonder if they know
I wonder why people are scared
"I don't look that scary, right?" I ask myself
Sometimes i agree with them
I wonder why i'm like this
Is it the way i act or look
I wonder all these things
But the question is why can't i wonder about the happy
things

I'm burning silently
Like an abandoned cigarette butt
Be careful because although I look ruined
I will set your world on fire

I hate the way I still feel your hands all over me
From head to toe, each shoulder hand and knee
For a long time, my life was built on a lie
Overpowered by manipulation and fear
So I kept quiet for what felt like hundreds of years
The secrets tore me up inside
With a twisted mind and arms tied
I grew up believing that it was my fault
My fault for every rape and every assault
Those dark cold memories haunt my brain
And sometimes I still feel I am the one to blame
Every night I lay awake
Wondering how much more of this I can take
How many times someone can say
"But it made you stronger babe"
I didn't need to be strong
I needed to be safe.
I needed someone to realise that I was in a dangerous
place
I needed someone to understand my silent pleas.

In the depths of the soul, a fire burns bright,
A light that flickers through the darkest of nights,
It's the spark of the spirit, the divine within,
A force that guides us through thick and thin.

It whispers to us in moments of peace,
In stillness, in silence, it brings us to release,
It's the voice of the universe, the song of the stars,
A rhythm that beats within our hearts.

It's the love that we feel, the compassion we show,
The kindness we offer to friend and foe,
It's the gratitude we hold, the joy we share,
The beauty we see in the world everywhere.

It's the faith that we have, the trust we believe,
The hope that we hold, the grace we receive,
It's the connection we make, the oneness we feel,
The awareness that everything is real.

So let us embrace this spiritual flame,
Let it guide us and light up our way,
For in the depths of the soul, a fire burns bright,
And it will lead us to eternal light.

I looked into a mirror
And I didn't see me
I saw the girl you created
And I hated it

Butterflies are beautiful. They wrap me in their warm home and hold me tight. Too tight. I start bleeding out bright red, colour spilling everywhere. I now know where butterflies get their colour and shine. I will be another mark on their wings. After all, butterflies are beautiful.

Amid the ebb and flow of time's embrace,
Echoes of eternity leave their trace,
In whispers of wind and shadows cast,
A journey of souls, from first to last.

The sands of existence, they slip away,
But within our hearts, they forever stay,
For in each heartbeat and whispered breath,
We find the symphony of life and death.

Good night, sleep tight
We're ethereal beings
We bathe in moonlight
Our nights spent dreaming
Our worries take flight

You snooze you lose

During the night he comes out
Crawling through your sheets
Shuts you up so you cannot shout
No one's safe from him
That pesky nocturnal beast
He's already started his feast
He feeds on our flesh
Til his insatiable hunger quenched

Lurking in the darkness
In the crevices he hides
He's beneath your sheets and
Whispers fears that gnaw inside
He's left forever marks in our hearts
Ugly scars on our sleeping skin
He's never really going to depart
He's already killed me within

Too late for a good night
It's too late to sleep tight
Too late, too late
We've let the bed bugs bite

If only
Our distance was the same as our minds
Closer than any other human.
Reading each other's thoughts,
With no hesitation.
Knowing each other
Like we grew up side by side
But have yet to touch
Have yet to lock eyes
Have yet to love properly
But still,
I find my way back
Aching for your love
Knowing it's wrong to ask
But finding my way back
You're not my drug, but i am yours
You are not bad for me,
But i am for you
I can't let you go because you are good
I am not
But I refuse to allow you to let me go
Because you are all that is holding me up

The Little Girl In Me

You have power over your mind - not outside events. Realise
this, and you will find strength
~ Marcus Aurelius

Note to self:
Stop trying to please everyone, it just makes you
miserable.

Our summer was a swirl of flavoured ice-cream
For you vanilla and me peach honey dreams
The beach we'd venture, a daily affair
Salty breeze tousling our hair

Missing buses and curfews ignored
Yet our smiles linger, our hearts unmoored
Late night talks under the starry dome
Late night walks, oh how far we roamed

Vanilla peach honey oh so sweet
More than the secrets we promised to keep
Vanilla ice cream melting off our tongues
The taste of peach lingers, sweet and young

The beach we went, Day by day
We swam in the sea, felt the sun's gentle sway
These few long days were utter bliss
Yet i waited each day for a single kiss

Vanilla's sweetness peach honey delight
We promise each other in the fading light
That we'll always love each other
But that wasn't right

What if I told you I loved you?
Would you take it full circle?
Accept it with grace?
Or stand there in silence?
Quietly laughing in my face
Would you say it back?
If the feelings were true
Or would you push me away?
Denying this news
Would you take me in?
Holding me close
Or turn away
When I need you the most
Would you press your lips to mine
So sweet to the taste
Or would you raise your hand
And cover your face
I don't know what I can offer
Don't know what I can do
But what I know is I can love you
And that is my honest truth

Love is not a term to use lightly
Yet I do it all the time
Self hatred is destructive
Yet I practise it religiously
I love adventure
But hate trying new things
I love life
Yet wish I weren't living it

Preaching is one thing and
Practising is another
Actions are lightning and well,
Words are just thunder

Yet people jump
When they hear the loud rumble
They think lightning is pretty
Won't cause them any trouble

Lightning is silent but deadly
And thunder is pretentious and proud
My mind is like lightning
And my words are just clouds

I didn't want to be your first choice
Because that implied that there was someone else
Someone you could love if you couldn't love me
Someone who would get every part of you that I so
desperately crave
I wanted to be the only one you could love

Please think before ever comparing our situations
Because I may have only drowned in the shower
Whereas you drowned in the ocean
But at the end of the day
Both of us drowned

You do not want a girl like me
I have scars hidden deeper than you can see
They are so deeply buried beneath skin
Do you want me to show you? Where would I begin?

Would you like me to start there or like me to start here
Would you like me to explain the meaning behind every
tear
Shall I uncover for you each scar from my past
Bring back the feelings I thought had finally passed

Do I start with the early years cause they were the first
Would you like that, would you like to hear the worst
It is a story I wish not to bestow
Would you act differently toward me after you know?

Maybe once you've listened and been able to see
Maybe only then you will understand why I am me
Only then you will realise why I act all cold
Learning each scar has a tale, a secret untold

Do you still see me the same way
Do you regret calling me gorgeous yesterday
Do you still see a woman that appears so strong
Or now do you scc a scarcd woman who has been tired
for so long

Would you still be able to fall for a woman like me
If I was vulnerable for only you to see
If I told you my innocence and purity were taken away
If stolen more than once, then would you stay?

Could you still hold me tight, and never let go
If I shared the hidden truth that happened years ago
Days turn into months and months into years
Slowly withering away, damp from my tears

Laying alone every night, fear became my friend
When would this stop? Where is the end?
I was just a young girl riddled with fear
My deep brown eyes shut when I knew they were near
I'd let out a tear, one that would always sting my cheek
For years and years it was a secret I did keep

Finally one day it all came out
From there, a passion did sprout
A passion to write
A passion borne purely out of anger and spite

For word by word, I spoke a painful truth
How a man I had trusted had stolen my youth
But I didn't care. I was finally making it right
He didn't care to stop when I had nightmares each night

He had taken so much and I was forced to see
From a young age life is a harsh reality
Behind closed doors, the truth was spoken
I appear to be grown but still, I'm a little girl who is just
broken

Broken by betrayal emotional victim of pain
But I've refused to let victim be part of my name
I am a warrior a survivor and I am not to blame

A warrior knows who she can trust
A warrior is courageous she is robust
And now you have heard me speak
Heard my story, my heart is yours to keep

But do you still want it, my heart in your hands the scars
you will see
Do you still want to fall for a woman like me
Do you still want to be there on my best days and worst
Now that I've bared my soul to show my deepest scar
first?

In the silence of the soul's expanse,
Where thoughts entwine and emotions dance,
Whispers of the heart arise, unseen,
A tapestry of dreams and memories glean.

The stars above, like echoes of the mind,
Glimmering secrets, stories entwined,
In the depth of night, truths unfold,
A universe of emotions, untold.

"But it made you stronger"
I WAS A FUCKING CHILD
I DIDN'T NEED TO BE STRONG I NEEDED TO BE
SAFE

Perhaps we will begin to put down our phones
And even learn to talk
Perhaps we will appreciate the smaller things
A cup of tea, a hug, a walk
Perhaps we'll begin to embrace each other
As if meeting anew
Perhaps we will learn to sacrifice
A little bit of 'me' for a little bit of 'you'

Perhaps we'll remember those who hid in years now
gone
By only candlelight
Perhaps we'll realise our misfortunes
Would insult those who lost that fight
Perhaps we'll begin to value our health;
That is a blessing and not a right
Perhaps we'll remind ourselves of this
Once the sickness is firmly out of sight

Perhaps we'll see the world with different eyes,
In all its chaos and splendour
Perhaps we'll see that life is something
To be enjoyed and not just to endure
Perhaps this will come to pass,
And perhaps we will learn a lot
But what i fear knowing us
Is perhaps we will not

In the concrete jungle where dreams are spun,
A woman weaves her tale, battles yet undone.
In the symphony of silence, her voice suppressed,
A poem for the women, society's oppressed.

In this labyrinth of expectations, she finds her way,
Dancing through glass ceilings, night and day.
The weight of judgments, a heavy load,
Yet she rises, fierce and bold.

She's more than a label, a stereotype to bear,
A warrior poet with stories to share.
In this society's grasp, she fights to be free,
Yearning for equality, a world where she can just be.

From catcalls on streets to the boardroom gaze,
She navigates a maze, caught in society's craze.
Her body, a battleground, a political war,
But she'll rise from the ashes, stronger than before.

In the whispers of locker rooms, she hears the hush,
Yet her resilience, a wildfire, a burning rush.
She's not just a statistic or a pawn in their game,
She's the phoenix in the ashes, reclaiming her name.

In classrooms and offices, where prejudice lingers,
She fights for her worth, with ten nimble fingers.

No longer confined to a prescribed role,
She's the anthem of rebellion, breaking the mould.

Her tears, a river, carved by the years,
But she's a storm, breaking through her fears.
For every glass ceiling that mocks her stride,
She'll shatter it with resilience, nowhere to hide.

It's hard to live in this world as a woman, it's true,
But with sisters in solidarity, the strength accrues.
In unity, a force that refuses to bow,
She stands tall, she stands now.

So, hear this slam, a battle cry loud,
For the women who fight, for the silenced, the proud.
In this symphony of struggle, let our voices soar,
For a world where living as a woman isn't a war.

Why did I have to fall in love with the sea?
He's calm with the breeze that refreshes my thoughts
I swim until I can't anymore and fall into his
surrounding embrace

When I panic he soothes me
When I cry my tears become a part of his ocean
I submerge myself in the water that surrounds me,
I dive deeper and deeper because I feel accepted

But sometimes the sea tries to drown me
I start sinking and wonder if I swam too far this time
Am I capable?
Or has someone else accomplished what I've been
attempting to do
All this time

The waves become big and everything that was once
beautiful turns into my enemy
How can I swim if the sea is my friend
But also my enemy?

The sea forgets about me and leaves me to die
So I rest sinking to the bottom
to just float back to the surface
Why am I in love with the sea

A Part Of Me

strength does not come from winning. Your struggles develop your strengths. When you go through hardships and decide not to surrender, that is strength
~ Arnold Schwarzenegger

I understand
Not only your body but your mind
Your spirit
Was violated by him

I understand
That he called you "pretty" first
And would hug you when you were scared
How he made you trust him

I understand
The sick feeling in your stomach
The swelling of your throat
the heat in your eyes
At the sight, sound and smell of him

I understand
The worry that they won't believe you
That they'll make excuses
That they'll say
You asked for it or
I can't see him doing that or
Boys will be boys or
What were you wearing
As if none of it is on him

I understand

How you didn't understand the severity right away
He was a friend
And maybe, just maybe, it was a misunderstanding
You trusted him

I understand
The guilt you feel
The blame you are putting on yourself
For his disgusting actions

I understand
The way you still feel his hands all over you
Even though you have sat in the shower hundreds of
times
Scrubbing them off
crying to the point you cannot see

I understand
The flashbacks
And the nightmares
And the way your mind disassociates from your body
The way your body shuts down because of him

I understand
That you think you are overreacting
It's been years

But all that can control your mind
All you can think about is him

I understand
How you wish you could go back to normal
Your body
Your mind
Your soul
How you wish it wasn't affected

I understand
The hidden messages you tried sending
And the subtle hints that you weren't ok
That you fought him
But were ignored and restrained

I understand
That there are so many things
You wish you'd done differently
Get up and run
That you weren't thinking straight
I hear your "no"
Your "stop"
Your cries for help
I feel your kicks
Your hands covering your body

So he couldn't put his hands up your shirt
Or down your pants

I understand
That you froze
That you didn't know what to do
How to react
Your mind left your body
Am I drugged?
I feel the tear running down your cheek
And the regret that you didn't do more
The "why didn't you fight back"
And the "you probably don't remember saying yes"
But you never gave consent to him

I understand
The way he held your hands so you couldn't fight back
The way he would say this is our secret game
The way he would tell you to try harder when you were
balling your eyes out
I feel the bruises he left
The pain all left by him

I understand
How all you want to do now is change
Dye your hair
Pierce your nose

So your body is one that was never taken advantage of
One that was never touched by him

I understand
How you feel disgusting
Because you still crave touch
You cope by being physically loved
Even though that is frowned upon
And makes what happened to you not as important

I understand
How you want to hurt him for what he did to you
Kill him
Torture him
Like he did you

I understand
That the anger in your heart
Is just a front for all the sadness you feel

I understand

I'm scared to love
I know it's bad
But I'm protecting myself
And I'm sorry for you trying to love someone broken like
me

I spoke to my saviour
My eyes wet with tears
I spoke rather harshly
And I laid out my fears
He responded with goodness
As only he can
Met my eye with mercy
And showed me his plan
He told me of heaven
Of his goals for my life
This didn't assuage me
It pierced like a knife
"I'm sinful and wretched,
I should have been damned!"
He spoke to me softly and held out his hand
But I could not take it
Guilt roared in my head
"Lord, what if I fail you?"
Then in a whisper he said
"Where would you fail
That I would not catch you?
Do you think I would let you
From the palm of my hand?
There is no place that I cannot reach you
You dwell in my kingdom, live on my land
Your road may be narrow but I will guide you
My angels guard every step that you take

I know this is hard, but remember my child
Your call of salvation was not a mistake
Of course you will stumble, but I am your Lord
I promise to lift you for this is my work.
So where would you fall to,
That I would not be
If you are to fall just remember,
You'll fall into me

Do you ever get sick of coming back?
'Cause I am sick of welcoming you
Forgiving the things you've done
Trusting your words, hoping for something new

You leave me on the lonely road
Knowing that i will stand and await your return
I wait until hope fades, then you reappear
Placing me in the same cycle, where arguments burn

Does the fear of losing me not pain your heart?
Does our shared time mean nothing at all?
I let you go when you sought a new life
But you constantly return, causing my heart to fall

I'm done with your toxic love
Erasing your existence from my life
I don't need your apologies or excuses
Keep your lies, I'm ending this strife

It wasn't her choice to grow up so fast
It isn't her fault she forgot what love is
It isn't her fault she finds peace in lies
It's all she's ever known
She kept breathing
Even with bullet holes in her lungs
She still carried all the weight
Even with stab wounds in her back
She is a fighter
Too bad it wasn't her choice
She is strong
Too bad she became that way by someone stacking all
their responsibilities on her back
She hates the idea of love
Only because she doesn't understand
Doesn't think she deserves it
If only someone had loved her right
If only someone showed her it's okay
Its ok to be vulnerable
Its ok to mess up
Don't cry my darling
It'll be over soon just wait

I don't think people realise how hard and tiring it is
Trying to explain how you feel
When you don't even understand it yourself

This too shall pass
~ Edward Fitzgerald

Before you place your judgement
May I add,
That you,
Do not understand
You were not there in that room,
Being told that God's love is conditional
That he does not love someone so sick,
So vile,
As you.
You do not understand
You were not in that room
Hearing those same words
Hearing the disgust, fear, judgement
You did not understand
You still don't
And I doubt you ever will
That I am less due to my experiences
We grew up with the same God
But you were taught unconditional love
And i was taught that our God has conditions
While I now know that the voice in that room was a lie
I still fail to part with the conditional love that God may
have for me
So again I ask
Before you speak any words on my faith
Ask yourself
Do you understand

I'm told that i'm good at making people feel heard and
seen,
Staying on the phone all night till the sun starts to peak.
I think i'm favourite on 20 different phones,
But something in me feels like a traitor, for the love that
I show.
I wonder when I'll get to be loved like them, whenever
that is.
I show just enough for my walls to look seemingly clear,
Unlike the words that I twist so my cries they'll never
hear.
"Can you talk?" "Can I rant?" what a true joy for me to
be asked.
But sometimes all it does is remind me of the last;
the last time someone asked me if i'm okay and tried to
know
I say that it reminds me, but I cannot remember
something that I do not know.
Does it feel good to have a person who's always there
and dries their tears?
Do they forget that the best comforters use just the words
that they wish to hear?
I know their love for me is real, they never want to leave
my side.
But something in me wonders if they just love the way I
lie

The version of me that you have created in your mind
Is not my responsibility

I long for the day where getting high meant the swing at the park again. When picking a flavour meant ice cream and lollies not drinks and vapes.
I long for the day i can call my father daddy again without it being sexualised by society and the day i can hug a boy without there being a motive behind it
I long for the day I put my phone down in the car and watch the raindrops fall down the window like they're racing again. The day where my biggest worry was if my crush got the love note i put in his lunchbox
I long for the day where "send" meant the 'among us' game code and all I knew about nude was that it's the colour my mum paints her nails.
I long for the day I laugh at my dads stupid jokes without rolling my eyes again. The day where I cartwheel and dance through the streets without worrying what others might think of me.
I guess I long for the day I wished away when I was little again.
I long for the day where I appreciate this innocence of 15. The day where I do not long for what yesterday and tomorrow hold. The day where I live in the now. Because when tomorrow comes i will wish i was in today again.
So maybe just maybe i should finally stop longing and start living

Sometimes you have to make peace with the fact that you're the villain in someone else's story, even if you thought you were doing the right thing. You don't get to tell them how to narrate their experience

The Desire In Me

Out of suffering have emerged the strongest souls; the most massive characters are seared with scars
~ Khalil Gibran

At every corner of the world
The seas always roar
Breaking and crashing on every country's shore
I walk on the soft yellow sand
My towel, shoes and heart in my hand
My new swimmers on
Ready to be worn
For the sea is the place I feel I am reborn
The waves violently crash on the old rocky dome
And now is when I finally realise the ocean is my home
The memories that are made at the beach
Are only adventures you experience
not ones you can teach
I dunk my head under the the sky blue water
Maybe the saying is true, like father like daughter
My dad he loves the ocean the water and the waves
Catching crabs is his favourite and exploring the caves
For we both love the sea as much as each-other
It's our home outside home
One we share with one another

If you don't heal from what hurt you
You will bleed on people that didn't cut you

The world is vast and full of wonder
A place where beauty and darkness thunder
We walk through life with heavy hearts
And search for meaning in all the parts

We seek the truth in every lie
And hope to find a reason why
But in the end, what do we find?
A world that's so cruel but also so kind
A place where joy and sorrow meet
I guess we can say life is bittersweet

We laugh and we cry, we love and we hate
And most of all we try to find our own fate
We make mistakes, but we learn and grow
And hope that someday we will know

The secrets of this world in which we live
And all the knowledge it can give
We strive for greatness, we aim for fame
And try to leave our mark on this huge complex game

But in the end, what does it mean
What is the point of this grand scheme
Is it all just a cosmic joke
Or something more profound more woke

perhaps it's up to us to decide
And find the meaning which is hidden deep inside
To live each day with love and grace
And find our own very special place

To cherish each moment spent
To find beauty in every second, every minute each event
To love with all our hearts and soul
And let our true sleeves take control

For life is short and oh so sweet
And every moment is a blessing, a gift, a treat
So let us live with joy and peace
And let our love and light increase

Let us take each day in stride
And find the beauty in the ride
For the road may be rough and steep
But it's the journey that makes life so deep

Behind the veil of illusions we tread,
In a world of masks, where truths are spread,
But peel back the layers, reveal the core,
And authenticity blooms, forevermore.

In a realm of whispers and shifting skies,
We seek the truth that beneath it lies,
Unravel the threads of falsehood's art,
And find the essence of every heart.

In the quiet depths where shadows play,
Echoes of time in endless sway,
Whispers of dreams that gently fade,
In the heart's chamber, secrets made.

A solitary star in the velvet night,
A silent tear that seeks the light,
In the dance of leaves, a whispered sigh,
In the stillness, truths silently lie.

In the river's flow, a timeless song,
In the embrace of dusk, where hearts belong,
A fleeting moment, a fleeting grace,
In the labyrinth of life, a fleeting chase.

Beyond the veil where thoughts entwine,
In the alchemy of love, where souls align,
In the silence between breaths untold,
In the whispers of eternity, stories unfold.

In the cosmos vast, where galaxies gleam,
In the symphony of existence, a cosmic dream,
In the array of fate, each thread we weave,
In the depths of being, in every heart's heave.

So listen closely to the symphony's call,
Feel the rhythm of life, each rise and fall,

For in every whisper, in every sigh,
Lies the depth of a soul, reaching for the sky.

Tears are the blood of the soul, they say,
A river of emotions that silently convey,
The depths of our joy or the weight of despair,
In each teardrop, a story, a burden to bear.

They flow from the heart, unbidden, untamed,
Carrying secrets and leaving trails unnamed.
In moments of sadness, they fall like rain,
Washing away sorrow, easing the pain.

In times of joy, they glisten like dew,
A reflection of happiness, a shimmering hue.
Tears speak the language our words cannot find,
They bridge the divide, connecting heart and mind.

They're a testament to our humanity's grace,
A tangible proof of the trials we face.
In vulnerability, our tears are our strength,
An emblem of courage, a journey's full length.

So let them flow freely, these tears from the soul,
Each drop makes us stronger and makes us whole.
In the tapestry of life, they play their role,
For tears are the blood of the spirit, a priceless toll.

From crawling to walking, we take our first steps,
With wide-eyed wonder, we embrace what's next.
Days turn into weeks, weeks into years,
Leaving us with childhood memories and a few tears.
It's hard to grasp how quickly it all goes,
Like sand slipping through our fingers, it flows.
From facing fears to making tough choices,
It's a journey that can sometimes drown out our voices.
The weight of expectations can feel so heavy,
As we strive to be successful and steady.
Balancing responsibilities, finding our way,
Gone are the days where we would just play.
Time flies by in the blink of an eye,
Growing up, it seems to just pass us by.
One moment we're kids, carefree and small,
Next, we're facing adulthood's call.

I think I can love you, I mean I can try
I can try and forget the past but i don't want to lie
Lie about the love that never stayed
Or try forget the consequences that both my heart and
soul paid
I promise to try my best, to love you like I should

If you avoid the conflict to keep the peace all you do is
create a warzone within yourself

Erasing everything I am writing right now
'Cause I don't know what to write about
It's not that I am running out of topics
But it's you, my heart wants to write about

It's 1:03am and
I am staring at the ceiling
Wishing it was that easy for me to say
Like you said, 'I just lost feelings'.

I wasn't even heartbroken
When you said it aloud
Because I was literally broken
When I saw you flirting around

And I gave you another chance,
Made the same mistake too many times
Still my heart wants to give you one last chance
Even though my brain denies it.

And I'm ready to make the same mistake,
Until I can call you mine
No matter how painful the process is
Because you once were the reason for my smile

I am not a victim for sharing my story
I am a survivor for sharing my story
A survivor for setting the world on fire with my truth

My skin without the scars it bares
Is like the night sky without the stars it wears

The Curiosity In Me

Life isn't about finding yourself. Life is about creating
yourself
~ George Bernard Shaw

What if i told you now
That fairy tales are lies
Every legend myth and story
All those that we live by

What if Aurora did not wish
To be touched while she would sleep
And that Persephone shrieked
consumed by darkness and grief

Their saviours became their captors
Gods turned into thieves
Princes turned into monsters
Forcing two lives to interweave

What if Psyches only options
Were either Eros or the Cliff
If these tragic romances
Are actually not all myths

What if Helen felt as trapped
As the Trojans did in war
Instead of a noose around her neck
A cursed oath she swore

What if good old Cinderella
Left her slipper as testimony

To remind to all that freedom
Was far greater than matrimony

What if Ariel did not choose
To sacrifice her whole identity
For a man who was not loyal
Her voice, her scales, and family

What if you found a speck of truth
In these treacherous words you read
And say "fuck fairy-tales" out loud
For they're as fucked up as fucked can be

I came across a little girl, one cold and windy day
A look of pain etched on her face, revealing her dismay.
I couldn't help but notice a tear fall on her cheek,
Her hands began to tremble, and her knees were growing
weak
She tried to part her lips and speak but nothing could be
heard,
A gasp of air escaped her mouth in place of any word
She fell down on her knees upon the cold and icy snow
As I draped her with my coat as the wind began to blow
She finally spoke with all the strength she had
"So much is going wrong for me i've lost the hope I had"
She folded both her hands and began to slowly pray
Looking for a miracle on that dark and gloomy day.
It only took a moment and a cloud began to part
A beam of light shot down and hit directly to her heart
Her body started glowing and that teardrop was erased
The smile forming on her lips, put joy back on her face
A puff of wind blew through her hair and I was struck in
awe
The beauty overtook me from this miracle I just saw
When she turned to look at me, it came as no surprise,
So deep in that reflection I saw Jesus in her eyes
She threw her arms around my neck embracing me with
love
Reminding me of the lessons that were sent from God
above

I pour my soul into these pages
Hoping it would give some release
To my head, that's been drowning me for ages
But I still can't find my peace

I just need to feel okay
But how? I think & think & think
Maybe it would be easier if someone would stay
But they all leave in a blink

Perhaps I push them away
I don't mean to
God why am I this way?
At this point I don't know what to do

Like a boat lost at sea
No land in sight
I scream for help, but no one's there, just me
I might give up on this flight

The waves would still crash
The sun would still rise
It would be over in a flash
No one cares about my demise

In the quiet echoes of the cosmic expanse,
Life unfurls, a dance, a fleeting chance.
A tapestry woven with threads of time,
A symphony composed in a rhythm sublime.

Love, the celestial force that binds,
A melody of hearts, where eternity finds.
In the vast theatre of existence, we play,
Our roles illuminated by love's soft ray.

Meaning, elusive, like whispers in the wind,
A quest through galaxies, where truths rescind.
Yet in the embrace of love, a purpose unfurls,
As life's kaleidoscope whirls and twirls.

In the twilight of moments, fleeting and brief,
Love transcends, a solace, a belief.
Through joy and sorrow, a constant guide,
In the labyrinth of life, love shall abide.

The meaning, a canvas painted with hues,
Reflections of love in the morning dews.
A journey through shadows, a quest to define,
The essence of life, in love, we entwine.

Through the cosmos, we wander and roam,
Seeking the meaning, the purpose, the home.

Yet in the quiet spaces between breaths,
Love whispers softly, transcending all deaths.

Life, a river flowing, seeking the sea,
Love, the current that sets the soul free.
In the tapestry of existence, woven above,
Life's true meaning is found in the embrace of love.

I'm tired of holding my heart in the palm of my hand
And giving my love to people who will never understand
How hard it is to walk while withering.
My mind in a jar and my hope in the grass;
Love from afar with my heart made of glass.

The right path, the wrong direction
The right love, the wrong affection
The right dream, the wrong connection
And a heartache that defies reflection

The right words, the wrong delivery
The right hope, the wrong recovery
The right puzzle, the wrong discovery
And a longing that won't set me free

The right moment, the wrong circumstance
The right song, the wrong dance
The right fire, the wrong chance
And a bittersweet, unfulfilled romance

The right puzzle, the wrong piece
The right love, the wrong release
The right longing, the wrong peace
And a love that will never cease

The right person, the wrong time
The right script, the wrong line
The right poem, the wrong rhyme
And a piece of you, lost in time.

Icarus, the daring son of Daedalus, so young,
To the sun, his waxen wings he evermore flung.
With feathers bound by mortal hands, he yearned to take
flight,
Ascending towards the fiery orb, a spectacle of pure
delight.

His father's wisdom cautioned, "Do not ascend too high,
For the sun's fierce rays will melt your wings, and you
shall die."
But Icarus, in youthful passion, soared to the boundless
sky,
Drawn by the sun's golden lure, reaching higher, oh so
nigh.

The wax began to soften, as he neared the sun's embrace,
His joy and wonder were undeterred by danger he
couldn't face.
Icarus, oh hapless child, reached the zenith of his flight,
His wings betrayed by arrogance, melting, dripping,
burning bright.

Downward he descended, no longer soaring high,
His once majestic wings reduced to ashes in the sky.
As Icarus fell, a lesson clear for all to see,
A touching tale of reckless pride and human frailty.

So remember, in your pursuits, your dreams, your art,
To temper ambition with wisdom, and let not arrogance
depart.
For like Icarus, who flew too close, too near the sun,
Vanity can lead to our downfall, leaving our hopes
undone.

In the stillness of the night, I hear a whisper's call,
A world unseen, a realm unknown, within the mind's
grand hall.
For in the silent corridors, where shadows seem to play,
I hear the echoes of a truth that sight cannot convey.

The symphony of secrets, in the quiet of the dark,
Reveals a universe of whispers, where dreams and
visions spark.
A subtle rustling of the leaves, a distant city's hum,
I listen to the world's secrets, as the night's enchantments
come.

Yet, 'tis not just with hearing that we glimpse the hidden
plane,
For sight, too, can unveil the unseen, a world beyond the
mundane.
In colours, shapes, and shifting forms, we find a deeper
art,
Where mysteries of existence dance, and meaning takes
its part.

A shadow on the wall, a glint within a gaze,
The world of vision weaves its spell, in myriad, mystic
ways.
In patterns and in constellations, the unseen finds its
sight,

As we peer into the depths of being, in the darkness and
the light.

So, in the union of the senses, where hearing meets the
gaze,
We journey through the hidden realms, in the wonder of
our days.
Hearing and seeing, hand in hand, they guide us on our
quest,
To fathom life's profoundest truths, in the heart's eternal
nest.

In hearing and in seeing, we explore the grand design,
And in the whispers and the visions, we find the soul's
true sign.
For in these senses, intertwined, we glimpse what lies
within,
A deeper, richer tapestry of existence to begin.

The mud beneath the ground must be wet
Because of all the water she cried.
But you grew a garden there for her
And you built a home with the things she said.

Have you ever wondered why she liked red?
Perhaps she bled through the rain that she awaited
But you left, aggressively scribbling in papers
That won't ever be touched again

Burning all of it with the cigarette butts; she melt.
Every monsoon she screamed louder, telling the thunders
how she felt.
What a scattered mind she owned, resembling the
lightning in the sky.
Asking the stars, "Are you dying or resurrecting?" "Was
it all a lie?"

You built a home for her and she reminded the sky that
it's undying.
You built a home for her and she lost her mind.
You built a home for her and she questioned why she
was desired.
You built a home for her and she was inspired to bring
all the rain, for, watering the garden
What you made for her was the only thing she wanted
alive.

In the quiet depths where emotions reside,
A wellspring of feelings, an unending tide.
I craft these words, an arras of grace,
To touch your heart, in this boundless space.

Through life's winding journey, we all must roam,
Seeking solace, finding our way back home.
In moments of joy or when tears softly weep,
In the silence of night, or when stars vigil keep.
Let's embrace the fragile, the tender, and strong,
The melodies of laughter, the cadence of song.
For deep within our souls, we find the sublime,
In every heartbeat, a rhythm, a rhyme.

In the warmth of a hug, in a lover's embrace,
In the smile of a child, in a wrinkled, wise face.
In acts of kindness and compassion so pure,
We discover the essence, the love that's secure.
The world may be complex, a thundering sea,
But in simple moments, we find what's meant to be.
Through trials and triumphs, we all leave our mark,
A journey of the soul, through the light and the dark.

So let this poem be a reminder, a guide,
To cherish each moment, to never let slide.
The beauty that surrounds us, the connections we share,
In the depth of life's tapestry, love's everywhere.

"What's the devil afraid of?" some may inquire,
In lands where darkness and temptation conspire.
A query that delves into the depths of the night,
To fathom the fears that shun the devil from light.

Not silver crosses or holy water's grace,
Nor sacred verses to slow down his pace.
For the devil's power knows no earthly bind,
But in the human heart, a secret we may find.
He trembles not at thunder, nor the howling gales,
Not even the fiercest of infernal tales.
The devil's dread hides in the flicker of hope,
In hearts that choose love over the darkness to cope.

He fears the kindness, the empathy that's found,
In the deepest compassion, in the gentlest of sound.
For love, like a beacon, a radiant ray,
Can chase away shadows and hold the night at bay.
The devil's afraid of a conscience clear,
Of redemption's whisper in the sinner's ear.
He fears the bonds of friendship and grace,
And the smiles that light up a compassionate face.

So, what's the devil afraid of? It's clear to see,
It's the warmth of love and humanity.
In the hearts that stand firm, that choose to believe,
The devil's afraid of the power to forgive.

Winter is on my tongue
I can feel the cold chill
The harsh wind in my bones
The cold no fire can fill

The Powerful Part Of Me

People will come into your life for a reason, a season, or
a lifetime.
~ Brian A. Chalker

We were strangers
Then friends
Then best friends
Until you betrayed me
And now we are strangers again
But strangers with memories

Old sensations surface
Rippling through my stomach
Reminders rendering me nervous
Result in a pending judgement

Swore it would be the last time
Foolishly hoping for a miracle
Suddenly addicted to a crime
Illusively a fellow criminal

A false satisfaction
Masks the growling hunger
A toxic attraction
Sends me rolling drunker

Stuck in a vicious spiral
A never ending cycle
Basking in denial
Failure a fitting title

Remember that it is okay to miss someone
But do not confuse that person with who they were
Or the memories you created together

I learnt in science
That every 7 years every single cell in your body is
replaced
And it relieves me to know that one day
I will have a body that you didn't touch

I asked God to remove all the distractions from my life
And only then is when I realised everything I thought I
had
Was nothing compared to what he has planned for me

Within the quiet chambers of solitude's grace,
We find the echoes of our innermost space,
Thoughts unfurl like petals of a hidden bloom,
A sanctuary where the soul finds room.

Amid the hush of whispers, we explore,
The depths of who we are at our core,
Embracing shadows and fragments long concealed,
In solitude's embrace, authenticity revealed.

The human mind is truly the scariest
thing of all,
A labyrinth of secrets, shadows on the wall.
In its vast space, mysteries lie in wait,
Dark corners where fears and desires congregate.

A land where dreams and nightmares interlace,
Thoughts in a dance, a never-ending chase.
Where hopes take flight on wings of fragile grace,
And in the abyss, our darkest demons we must face.

Innocence and cruelty, both coexist within,
A battleground of conscience, a war we fight to win.
Within this fragile vessel, thoughts like wildfire spread,
The power to create or destroy, to heal or leave us dead.

The human mind, a universe so vast and deep,
Where secrets and desires in silent slumber sleep.
It holds the keys to worlds that none but we can know,
A place where both our greatest strengths and
weaknesses grow.

Yet in this boundless space, we find our greatest art,
The power to empathise, to love, to heal the heart.
For in the human mind, where our complexities reside,
Lies the potential to conquer fear and cast darkness
aside.

So though the human mind may be a fearful thing,
With shadows and with doubts that constantly cling,
It also holds the light, the hope, the will to rise,
To see beyond the fear, and reach for clearer skies.

In a world where stories endlessly unfold,
A tale of words, a poem to be told.
With verses that weave through the fabric of time,
Let's embark on a journey, in rhythm and rhyme.
From the dawn of existence to the present day,
Humanity's epic, in a poetic display.
Let us delve into the records of history's tome,
In this tapestry of words, let the verses roam.

In ancient lands where legends began,
The tales of heroes, of women and man.
From Gilgamesh's quest to the gods' grand design,
To the odyssey of Homer, in verse so divine.
The pyramids rose, with secrets untold,
And pharaohs ruled with crowns of gold.
In the sands of time, where the Sphinx doth lay,
Egypt's enigma mystifies to this day.

Greece, the cradle of philosophy's birth,
Socrates, Plato, Aristotle's worth.
In the groves of Athens, where wisdom did gleam,
A legacy of thought in the poet's dream.
The Roman Empire, its mighty reign,
From the Colosseum to the Appian Plain.
With Caesar and legions, the crowns of leaves they wore,
In epic battles, their destinies swore.

The mediaeval tapestry, a canvas so vast,
With knights and castles, a chivalrous past.
In the tales of Arthur and his noble quest,
Camelot's legend, in history's chest.
The Renaissance bloomed, a cultural revival,
With da Vinci's art, and the Bible's arrival.
Shakespeare's quill, in poetic array,
Crafted sonnets and plays that still hold sway.

Through the ages, in revolutions and strife,
Nations rose, empires fell from life.
From revolutions' cry to the battles they waged,
Freedom and rights, in history's page.

The industrial age, with progress's might,
Steam engines and factories, a brilliant sight.
Inventions and innovations, a world transformed,
With dreams in the heart, and hope in the storm.
The 20th century, with its joys and despair,
Two World Wars and the moon's distant glare.
The rise of technology, a global connection,
In the midst of turmoil, a human reflection.

And now, in the present, we stand hand in hand,
In a world that's equally fragile and grand.
With challenges and dreams, our journey's yet long,
In the verses of life, we all do belong.

In this poem, we've travelled through history's maze,
With its stories and legends, in poetic praise.
The world is a canvas, with stories untold,
In the tapestry of life, where our verses unfold.

Love is…

The way
the sun sets
So the moon can shine

Love is…

The way
The leaves change colour
To welcome autumn

Love is…
The way
I left you
even though I loved you

It's wrong to say I fell in love with you because I didn't
fall
If anything I ran willingly into ur arms
Your cold cold arms that somehow bring so much
warmth to my heart
So it's safe to say I wish I fell because in saying that
I could prove that the choice was not mine to love you

Eyes are loud,
The voice in his eyes is deeper than his actual voice
His eyes could make someone as vulnerable as me fall in
love with him
I somehow look prettier in the reflection of his eyes
I love how they hide when he smiles
I love how they give me a look when i say something
dumb
I love the warmth I feel when he's just looking at me
I love how my heart beats faster when our eyes collide
I love his eyes
How loud they are
But how they bring silence to my mind

Her wings heavy, her voice stolen
Her halo tarnished, no longer golden
She dances on the edge of despair
I guess life is just never fair
Between heavens harsh hiss
And hell's sweet kiss
She whispers secrets into the abyss

Hell is a teenage girl they say
Smoking into a dirty ashtray
Laughter echoes into screams
All the remains of failed dreams
Demons for days and shadows of shame
Haunted by memories which'll never tame
Cursed by the rage from within
Torn between innocence and the allure of sin

Now she sinks deeper into the abyss
of her own bloody creation
And gives the cruel world one final kiss
Her eyes tired and her wings are cold
She joins the rest of the stories now left untold

Acknowledgement

Writing this book has been a journey of discovery and growth, and I am deeply grateful to everyone who has supported me along the way.

First and foremost to my mother Foutine Ardeleanu, thank you for being my best friend, we don't always see eye-to-eye, but without you I would not be here today. Never doubt your greatness. You have shown me the mother that I wish to be someday. I love you endlessly

To all the amazing men in my life, thank you for showing me all the love in the world. To my father, thank you for always treating me like a princess, To my Poppy (aka my favourite person ever) I will never forget everything you do for me from buying me berries to taking me around the world. I love you, for my awesome uncles: Brook and Matt, thank you for being the best uncles I could ask for, showing me the way a woman should be loved and loving me endlessly. And finally to my brother, I don't know where to begin but to save the cost of printing an extra 10 pages per book I will say this, thank you for making me smile and laugh like an idiot, thank you for the kisses you give me when I'm sad and the youtube shorts you send me when I need cheering up, you will always be my baby brother and I will always be your big sis, I will forever be your biggest advocate and your number 1 admirer, never stop being awesome my love.

To Alberta Noden, I owe a debt of gratitude, you are not only my editor but my Godmother, my aunty and my cheerleader,

you have a special place in my corner watching others come
and go, but you sit there with your coffee and your cross
stitching and for your constant support I am forever grateful.

A special thank you for all the women who have helped shape
my mind into one that loves, Stacey Admiral, Dr Lakmali
Edirimanne and Jessica Cabral without your professional help
the young woman who now stands before you would be very
different

To my beautiful Aunty Drea, although distance may separate
our hearts will always be together. I am so grateful for the
memories you have created with me. Thank you for always
reminding me to be my own person (a strong one). I love you

For Cassandra Collier, my guide, my example and my
shoulder to cry on, thank you for being a second mother for
me, loving me like your own and never giving up on all my
hopes and dreams (especially the crazy ones)

For Ma, I know you're watching me from your seat up in
heaven and I hope I am making you proud, I will never stop
missing you and the crazy life I live I live to honour you.

To all the awesome people in my life if your name isn't in here
please know that it is in my heart.

Lastly, to the readers who will journey through these pages,
your interest in this work is deeply appreciated. I hope this
book inspires and informs as much as it has enriched my own
understanding.

Thank you all for being part of this incredible adventure.